REPTILES

R E P T

Black Caiman

Melanosuchus niger

SOUTH AMERICA

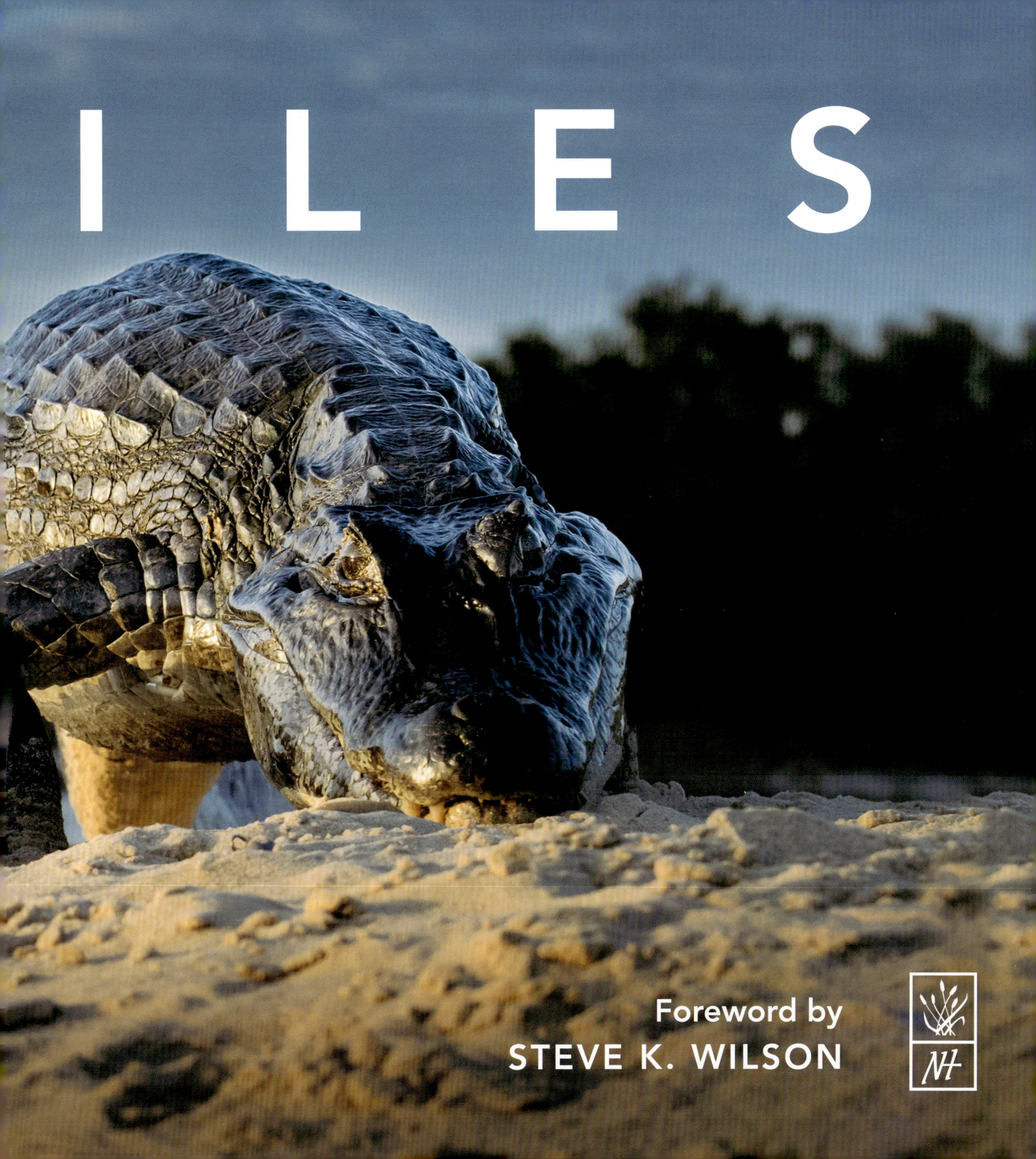
ILES
Foreword by
STEVE K. WILSON

WHY REPTILES?

The images in this book celebrate the beauty and marvellous design of some of our most misunderstood animals, the reptiles. They share a magnificence and elegance that we are now beginning to really appreciate. They are, in the true sense of the word, awesome!

The images have stories to tell. A gecko with padded toes dashes across vertical glass, seeming to mock the laws of gravity as it moves effortlessly over that smooth surface. In just a fraction of a second a chameleon unleashes its tongue, a high velocity projectile, with the accuracy of a marksman to snatch an insect from a twig a body's length away. In a powerful test of strength and endurance, two great Komodo Dragons, the largest living lizards, rise on their hind limbs and try to topple each other in a meeting of muscles and scaly hides. A crocodile lunges from murky waters that are clearly too dangerous for man or beast to enter, and seizes a migrating wildebeest, its toothy jaws easily capable of snapping the mammal's limbs. And as the sun's rays slant through clear tropical sea, a turtle propels itself forward slowly and elegantly with lazy movements of its flippers.

A GREAT DIVERSITY

There are 12,000 described species of reptiles, a number that continues to climb each year as more are discovered and named. Such diversity, and their presence on all continents except Antarctica, speaks volumes about reptiles as an ongoing success story. They are often the most abundant vertebrates in many habitats.

Reptiles have adapted to thrive over most of the Earth's surface. They are even in the oceans. Sea turtles remain obligated to land, where they must haul themselves up to lay eggs. However, the true sea snakes have completely severed all terrestrial bonds. They are born alive in the sea, and thanks to paddle-shaped tails, valvular nostrils placed on the tops of their snouts, and an ability to secrete surplus salt, they never willingly leave the water.

Reptiles are most successful in tropical rainforests and deserts, where dozens of species often occur side by side. In the forest canopy snakes scarcely thicker than string lie in ambush, virtually weightless among leaves and thin branches, while on the ground in perpetual damp, reptiles lurk beneath the rotting logs or bask in puddles of dappled sunlight.

Many desert reptiles avoid the extreme heat by foraging at night and sheltering by day in well-insulated burrows. Some have even evolved shovel-shaped snouts, so they can move with ease through loose sand as if it were fluid.

DEBUNKING THE MYTHS

The greatest myth is the perception of reptiles as the poor cousins of superior, more modern mammals and birds. With an evolutionary history spanning more than 200 million years, reptiles clearly exhibit functional designs that are both effective and enduring. Turtles and crocodiles have persisted relatively unchanged over that period. Yet there is abundant evidence of other groups, including some lizards, rapidly evolving when faced with changing circumstances such as isolation, new competitors and altered habitats. Reptiles are simultaneously ancient and dynamic.

Reptiles are no longer regarded as 'cold-blooded' creatures enslaved by the vagaries of the weather and locked into redundant designs while new improved, advanced vertebrates evolved.

It is true that, for the most part, reptiles do not generate their own body heat and cannot normally remain active in cold conditions. In contrast, mammals and birds have in-built internal heating systems allowing them to generally function year-round in all climates. But these are just different options, each with pros and cons.

Reptiles are very cheap to run. Depending on species and circumstances, meals may be days or weeks apart. For mammals and birds, operating an internal thermostat requires a daily and sometimes hourly feeding regime. They can remain fully active in icy weather but it is much more expensive.

As ectotherms, reptiles source their heat externally. But they can adjust their temperatures with precision by basking, and shifting between sun-warmed surfaces and cooler shady sites. They can orient their postures to expose more surface area to the sun or align themselves into its rays to reduce excess. Some even adopt daily colour regimes, starting the morning with dark, heat absorbent hues and shifting to pale reflective tones as the temperature rises. Even the simple tubular shape of a snake can be radically modified by stretching and flattening or tightly coiling to acquire and retain heat.

Many reptiles actually have preferred operating temperatures much higher than our own. They function effectively at levels which, in humans, would trigger heat stroke. Yet other cool-climate specialists can overheat if held in a human hand.

SUPER SENSES

Reptiles perceive their world using sophisticated senses, some of which are quite foreign to us. Some can see in the ultraviolet spectrum, others employ chemical cues to navigate their environment, and many snakes have evolved state-of-the-art thermal imaging.

Eyesight is important for most species, as it is for humans. Some lizards have strategically placed colours on throats, flanks and even bellies that can be flashed to potential mates and rivals using nods and dips of the head and tilting of the body. These are visible in the ultraviolet spectrum that we cannot see. They broadcast information about territorial and sexual status on a pallet easily visible to their own kind but obscured from predators overhead.

Among the tropical foliage of South-East Asia, where whip-thin and well-concealed vine snakes hunt swift, agile lizards, a missed strike is a lost meal. For these snakes accurately assessing distance is critical, and they have some of the most highly evolved visual acuity among snakes. They have binocular vision. The scope of each eye overlaps, and to achieve this their eyes are large and their snouts are slender with a groove running from eye to tip. They also have a unique keyhole-shaped pupil and densely packed receptors at the rear of the retina, focusing the sharpest vision directly ahead.

Pit vipers, pythons and boas have mastered the art of thermal imaging. Heat sensory pits between the eye and nostril of pit vipers and on the snouts and lips of pythons and boas allow them to detect infra-red radiation. Sensitive to a fraction of a degree Celsius, they can be used to precisely determine the direction and distance of the heat source of an animal such as a mouse, allowing an accurate strike, even in the absence of light.

Many reptiles explore their surroundings and detect food, threats or mates using chemical markers. The deeply forked, constantly flickering tongues of snakes and monitor lizards are clearly visible in some of the pictures in this book. They are part of a fine-tuned chemical analysis plant. Minute particles are collected and transferred to a cavity in the roof of the mouth called Jacobson's organ where they are identified. Different loads on each fork of the tongue help determine the direction of a source.

REPTILES IN TROUBLE

Most of us are familiar with reptiles because they often thrive in our midst. Lizards bask in the sun along the edges of our gardens, turtles paddle in ornamental ponds and we sometimes chance upon snakes when we walk in local forests.

Sadly many reptile species are not doing so well. We fear some have become extinct in recent years and others are on the brink. Some are listed as endangered and critically endangered, requiring careful management to conserve them. They face the same threats as other animal and plant species: habitat loss and fragmentation, persecution and the increasing spectre of climate change.

There is also the growing insidious trade in wildlife trafficking. Attractive, unusual and rare species are often highly desirable as pets. Smuggled from the point of capture to global markets, the animals have a poor survival rate during transit. However those that make it can fetch high prices, further fuelling the trade.

It is hoped that this book shines a light on our reptilian friends, and most importantly a desire to conserve and protect them. Not just for future generations of humans to enjoy, but for their own sake as well. After all, reptiles have been here for 200 million years!

Steve K. Wilson

Wagler's Viper

Tropidolaemus wagleri

ASIA

Southern Leaf-tailed Gecko

Saltuarius swaini

AUSTRALIA

Nile Crocodile

Crocodylus niloticus

SUB-SAHARAN AFRICA

Asian House Gecko

Hemidactylus frenatus

PAN-TROPICAL

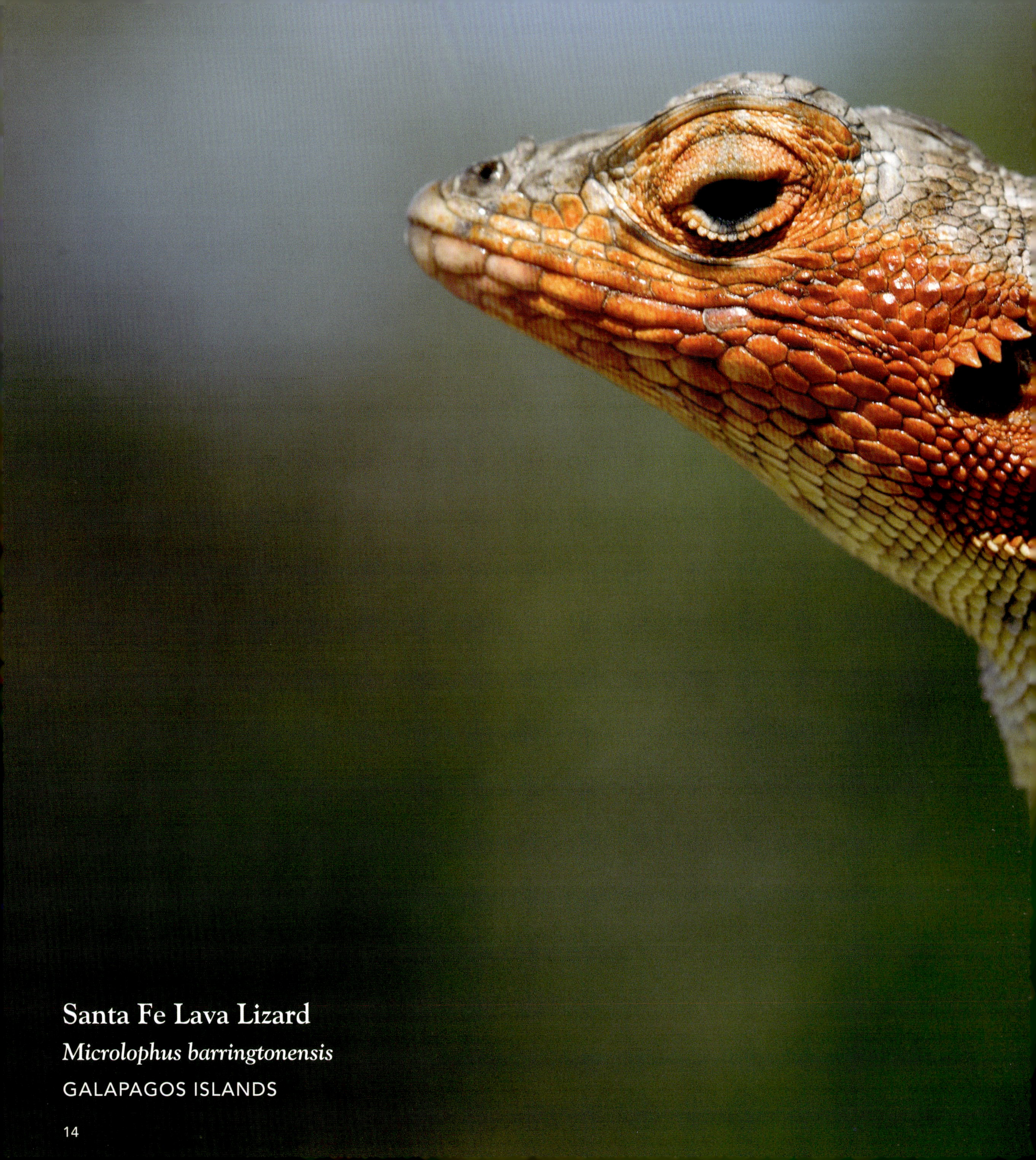

Santa Fe Lava Lizard

Microlophus barringtonensis

GALAPAGOS ISLANDS

Spectacled Caiman

Caiman crocodilus

SOUTH AMERICA

Komodo Dragon

Varanus komodoensis

INDONESIA

Green Python

Morelia viridis

AUSTRALIA AND NEW GUINEA

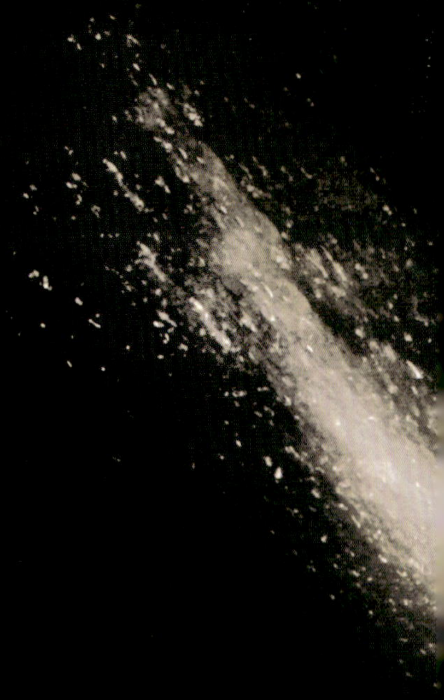

Marine Iguana

Amblyrhynchus cristatus

GALAPAGOS ISLANDS

Western Diamondback Rattlesnake

Crotalus atrox

USA

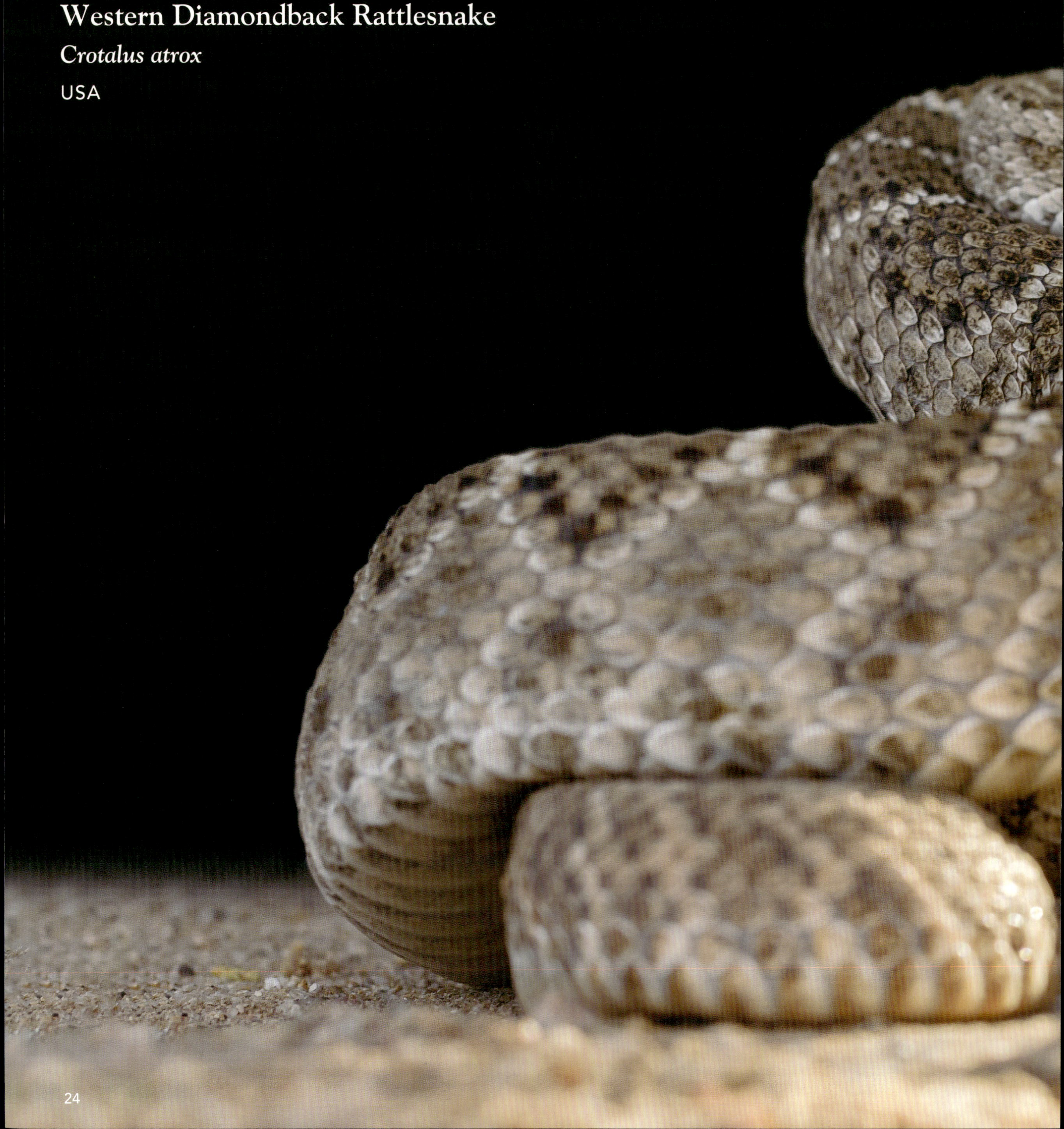

Black Mamba

Dendroaspis polylepis

AFRICA

Spear-point Leaf-tailed Gecko

Uroplatus ebenaui

MADAGASCAR

Green Sea Turtle

Chelonia mydas

OCEANS WORLDWIDE

Painted Bronzeback

Dendrelaphis pictus

SOUTH-EAST ASIA

Krefft's River Turtle

Emydura krefftii

AUSTRALIA

Green Anole

Anolis carolinensis

USA AND CARIBBEAN

Chameleon Forest Dragon

Gonocephalus chamaeleontinus

SOUTH-EAST ASIA

Panther Chameleon

Furcifer pardalis

MADAGASCAR

Yellow-lipped Sea Krait

Laticauda colubrina

INDIAN AND PACIFIC OCEANS

Crested Gecko
Correlophus ciliatus
NEW CALEDONIA

Argentinian Boa

Epicrates alvarezi

SOUTH AMERICA

Cottonmouth

Agkistrodon piscivorus

USA

Namib Rock Agama

Agama planiceps

SOUTHERN AFRICA

Freshwater Crocodile

Crocodylus johnstoni

AUSTRALIA

Red Worm Lizard

Amphisbaena alba

SOUTH AMERICA

Brown Anole

Anolis sagrei

MEXICO AND CARIBBEAN,
WIDELY INTRODUCED ELSEWHERE

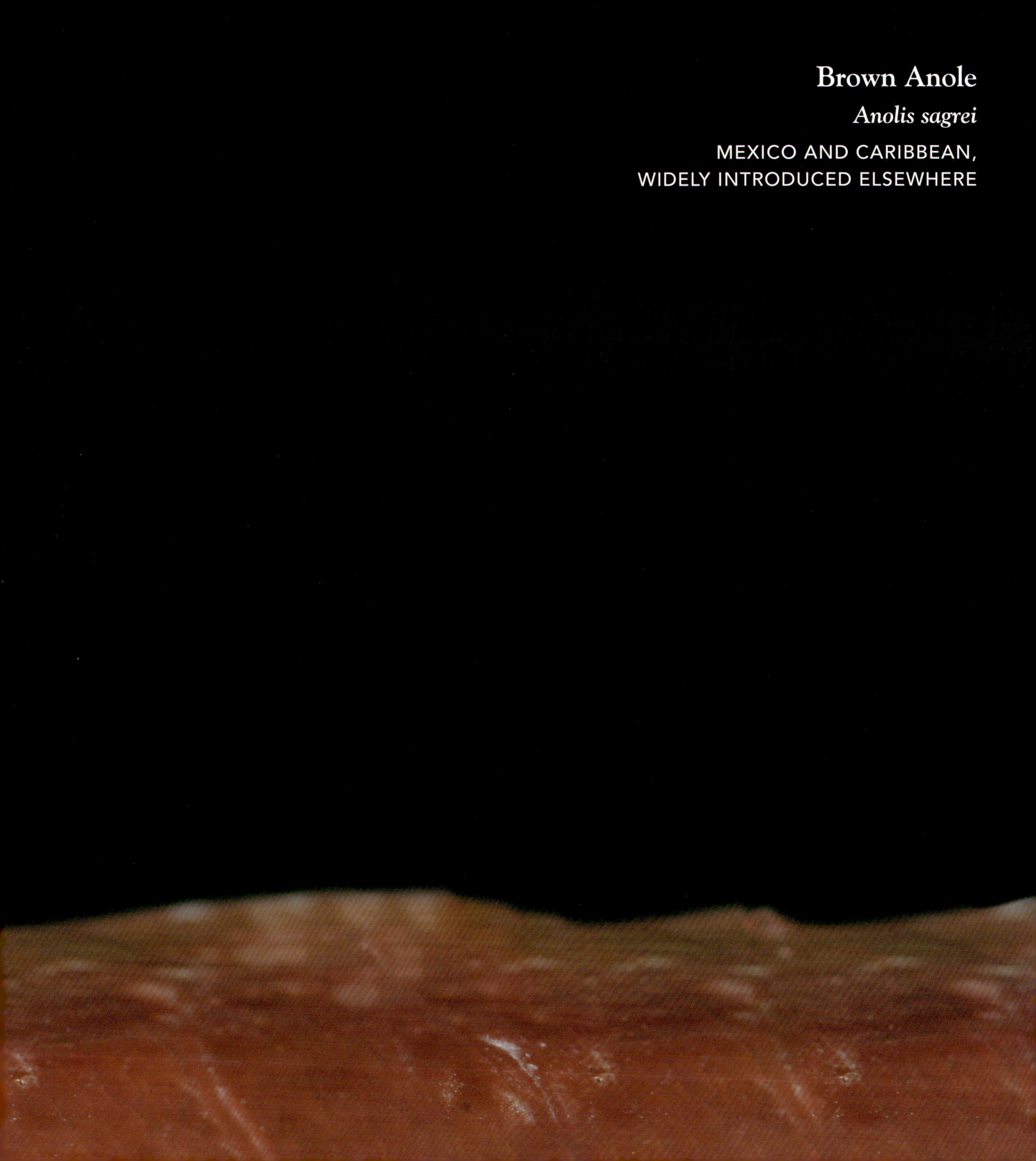

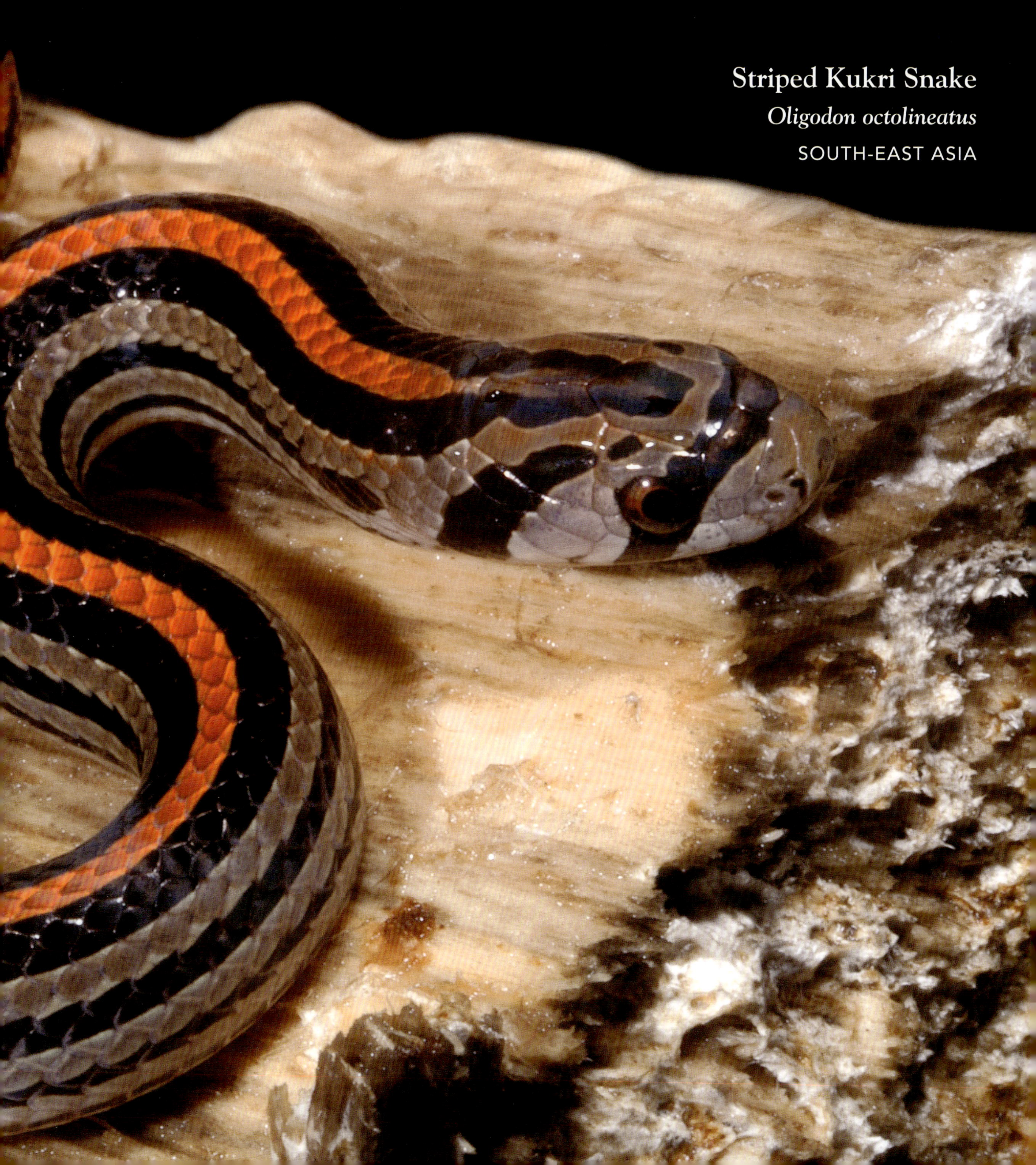

Striped Kukri Snake

Oligodon octolineatus

SOUTH-EAST ASIA

Carrot-tail Viper Gecko

Hemidactylus imbricatus

SOUTH ASIA

Boomslang

Dispholidus typus

AFRICA

Eastern Bearded Dragon

Pogona barbata

AUSTRALIA

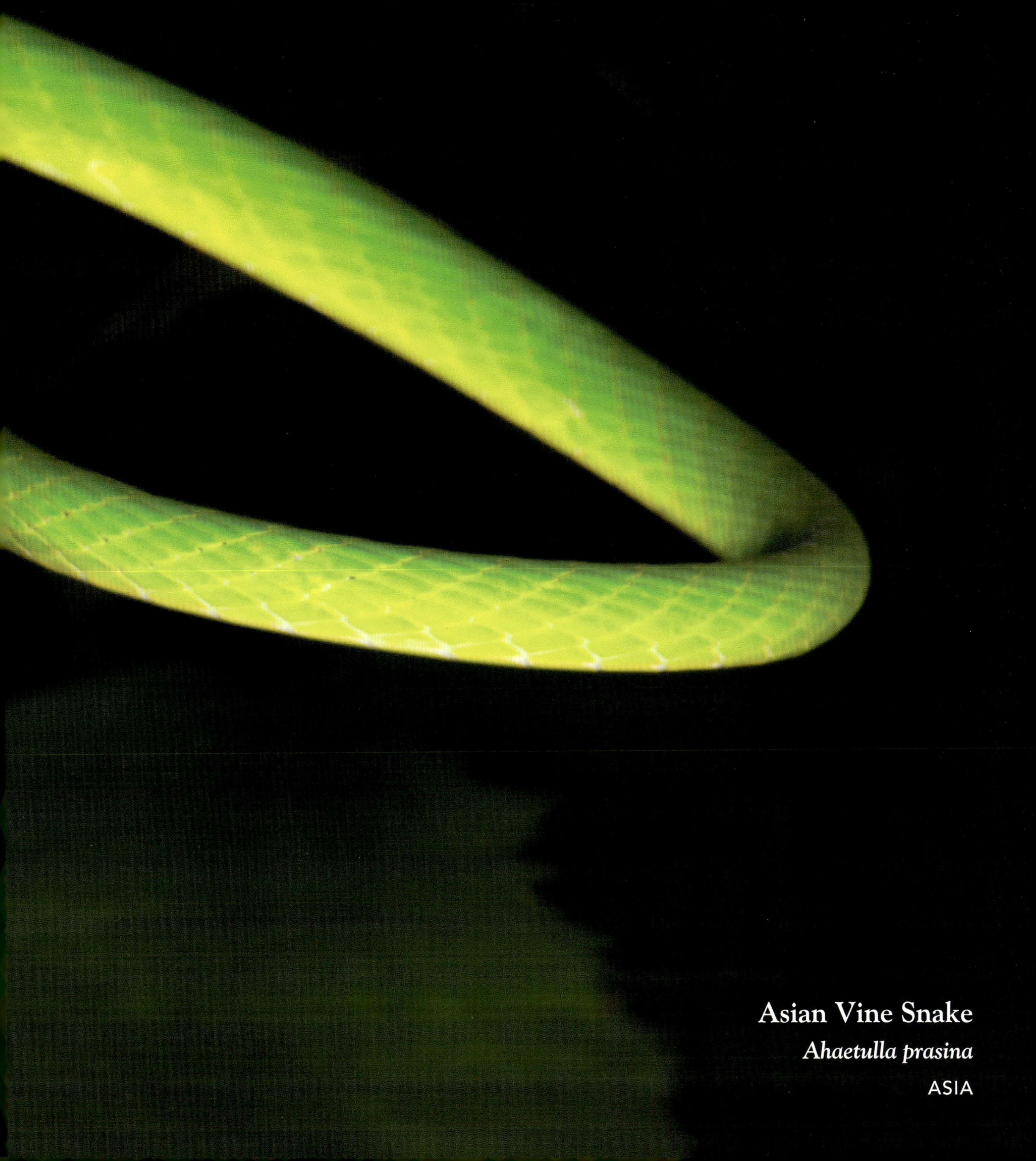

Asian Vine Snake

Ahaetulla prasina

ASIA

Blue-legged Chameleon

Calumma crypticum

MADAGASCAR

Red-footed Tortoise

Chelonoidis carbonaria

SOUTH AMERICA

Biak Tree Monitor

Varanus kordensis

INDONESIA

Mangrove Snake

Boiga dendrophila

SOUTH-EAST ASIA

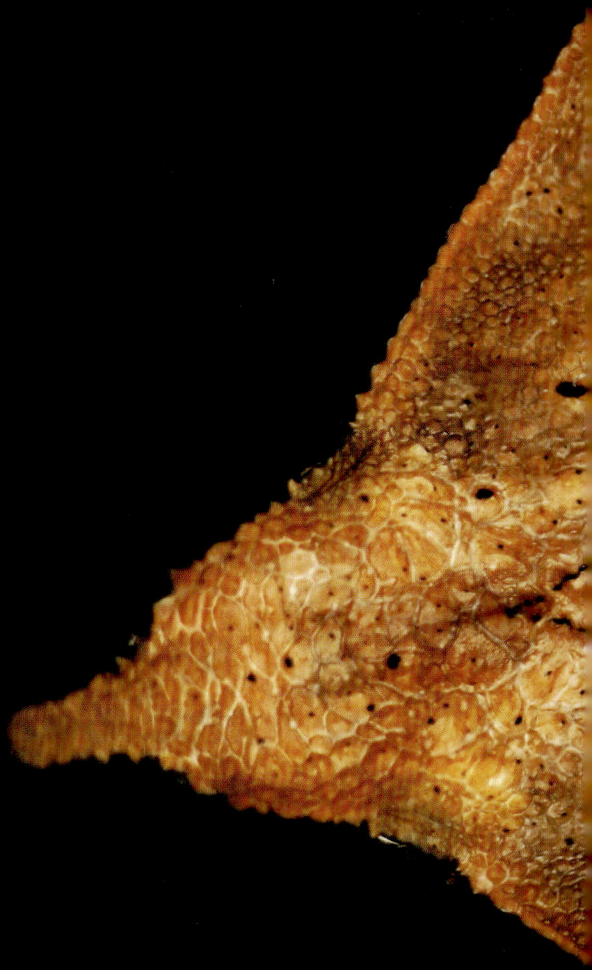

Matamata Turtle

Chelus fimbriata

SOUTH AMERICA

White-lipped python

Leiopython species

NEW GUINEA

Green Iguana

Iguana iguana

CENTRAL AMERICA AND SOUTH AMERICA,
WIDELY INTRODUCED ELSEWHERE

Sunda White-lipped Pit Viper

Trimeresurus insularis

INDONESIA

Indian Star Tortoise

Geochelone elegans

INDIAN SUBCONTINENT

Muller's Skink

Sphenomorphus muelleri

INDONESIA

Common Adder

Vipera berus

EURASIA

Bent-toed gecko

Cyrtodactylus species

ASIA

Cooper Creek Turtle

Emydura krefftii emmotti

AUSTRALIA

Sand Boa

Eryx colubrinus

AFRICA

Hermann's Tortoise

Testudo hermanni

EUROPE

Amazon Whipsnake

Chironius carinatus

SOUTH AMERICA

European Glass Lizard

Pseudopus apodus

EURASIA

Rough-scaled Python

Morelia carinata

AUSTRALIA

Indochinese Spitting Cobra

Naja siamensis

SOUTH-EAST ASIA

Red-eared Slider

Trachemys scripta elegans

USA AND MEXICO,
WIDELY INTRODUCED ELSEWHERE

Dwarf Caiman

Paleosuchus palpebrosus

SOUTH AMERICA

Mexican Horned Pit Viper

Ophryacus undulatus

MEXICO

Santa Fe Iguana

Conolophus pallidus

GALAPAGOS ISLANDS

Jackson's Chameleon

Trioceros jacksonii

EAST AFRICA

Rhinoceros Viper

Bitis nasicornis

AFRICA

Eastern Spiny-tailed Gecko

Strophurus williamsii

AUSTRALIA

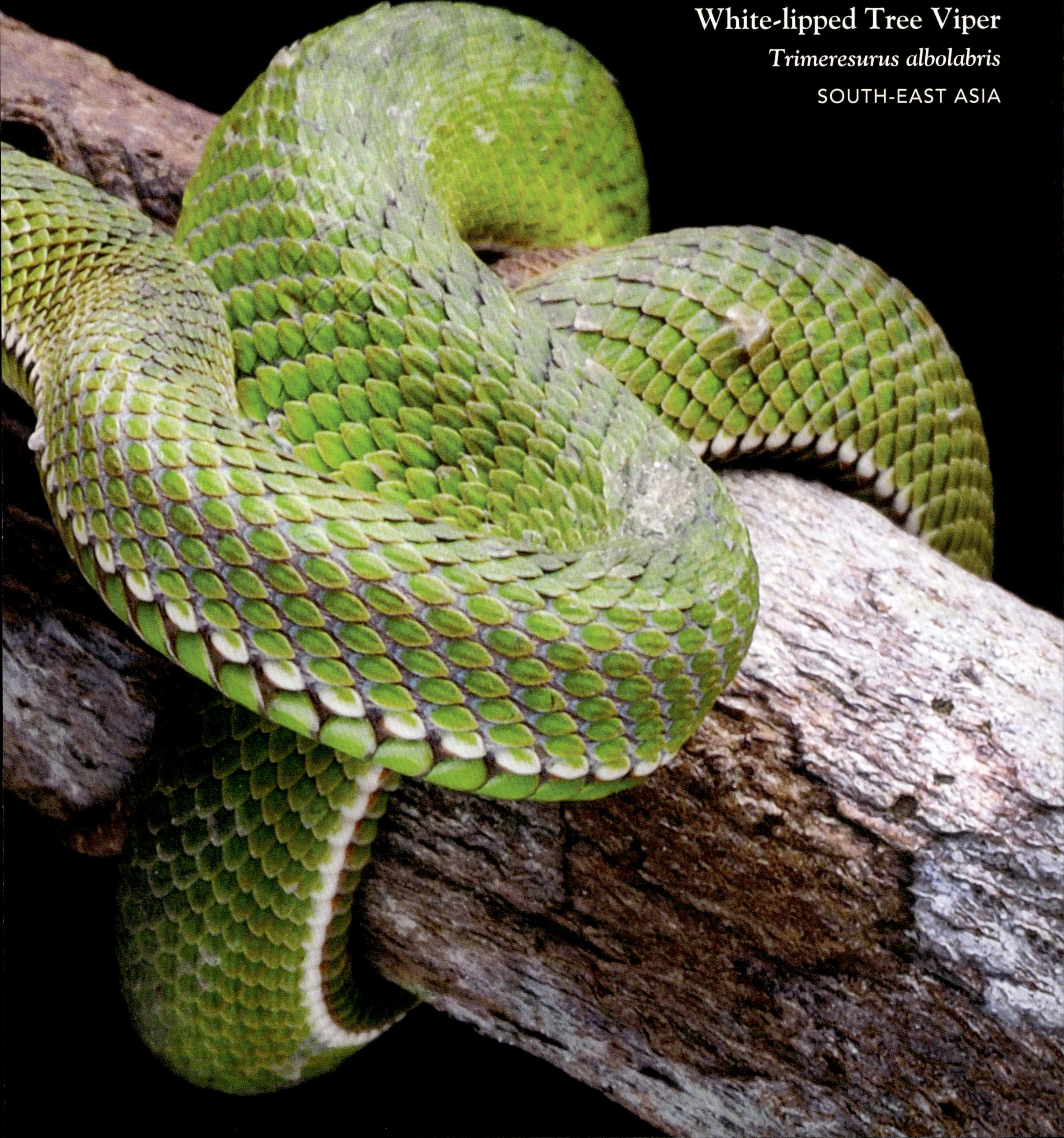

White-lipped Tree Viper

Trimeresurus albolabris

SOUTH-EAST ASIA

Lace Monitor

Varanus varius

AUSTRALIA

Veiled Chameleon

Chamaeleo calyptratus

ARABIAN PENINSULA

Tokay Gecko

Gekko gecko

ASIA

Peringuey's Viper

Bitis peringueyi

SOUTH-WEST AFRICA

Red-eyed Crocodile Skink

Tribolonotus gracilis

NEW GUINEA

Southern African Python

Python natalensis

CENTRAL AND SOUTHERN AFRICA

Prickly Knob-tailed Gecko

Nephrurus asper

AUSTRALIA

Guyana Root Tegu

Loxopholis guianense

SOUTH AMERICA

Malagasy Giant Hognose Snake

Leioheterodon madagascariensis

MADAGASCAR

Gharial

Gavialis gangeticus

INDIAN SUBCONTINENT

Brahminy Blindsnake

Indotyphlops braminus

PAN-TROPICAL

Shingleback

Tiliqua rugosa

AUSTRALIA

Yellow Anaconda

Eunectes notaeus

SOUTH AMERICA

Schmeltz's Rainbow Skink

Carlia schmeltzii

AUSTRALIA

Banded Krait

Bungarus fasciatus

SOUTH ASIA

Black-and-white Tegu

Salvator merianae

SOUTH AMERICA

Giant Horned Lizard

Phrynosoma asio

MEXICO

New Guinea Snake-Lizard

Lialis jicari

NEW GUINEA

Green Rat Snake

Gonysoma prasinum

SOUTH ASIA

Tuatara

Sphenodon punctatus

NEW ZEALAND

Halmahera Sailfin Dragon

Hydrosaurus weberi

INDONESIA

Common Green Racer

Philodryas viridissima

SOUTH AMERICA

Thorny Devil
Moloch horridus
AUSTRALIA

Carpet Python

Morelia spilota mcdowelli

AUSTRALIA

European Pond Turtle

Emys orbicularis

EURASIA

Kristin's Spiny-tailed Gecko

Strophurus krisalys

AUSTRALIA

Frilly House Gecko

Hemidactylus platyurus

ASIA

Cape Dwarf Chameleon

Bradypodium pumilum

SOUTH AFRICA

Pig-nosed Turtle
Carettochelys insculpta
AUSTRALIA AND NEW GUINEA

Day gecko

Phelsuma species

INDIAN OCEAN ISLANDS

Common Basilisk

Basiliscus basiliscus

CENTRAL AMERICA AND SOUTH AMERICA

Thorn-tailed Gecko

Strophurus assimilis

AUSTRALIA

Madagascar Girdled Lizard

Zonosaurus madagascariensis

MADAGASCAR

Ornate Earless Agama

Aphaniotus ornata

BORNEO

Eastern Crevice-Skink

Egernia mcpheei

AUSTRALIA

Western Black Tree Snake

Thrasops occidentalis

AFRICA

Frilled Lizard

Chlamydosaurus kingii

AUSTRALIA

Common Leopard Gecko

Eublepharis macularius

SOUTH ASIA

Rough-scaled Brown Skink

Eutropis rudis

SOUTH-EAST ASIA

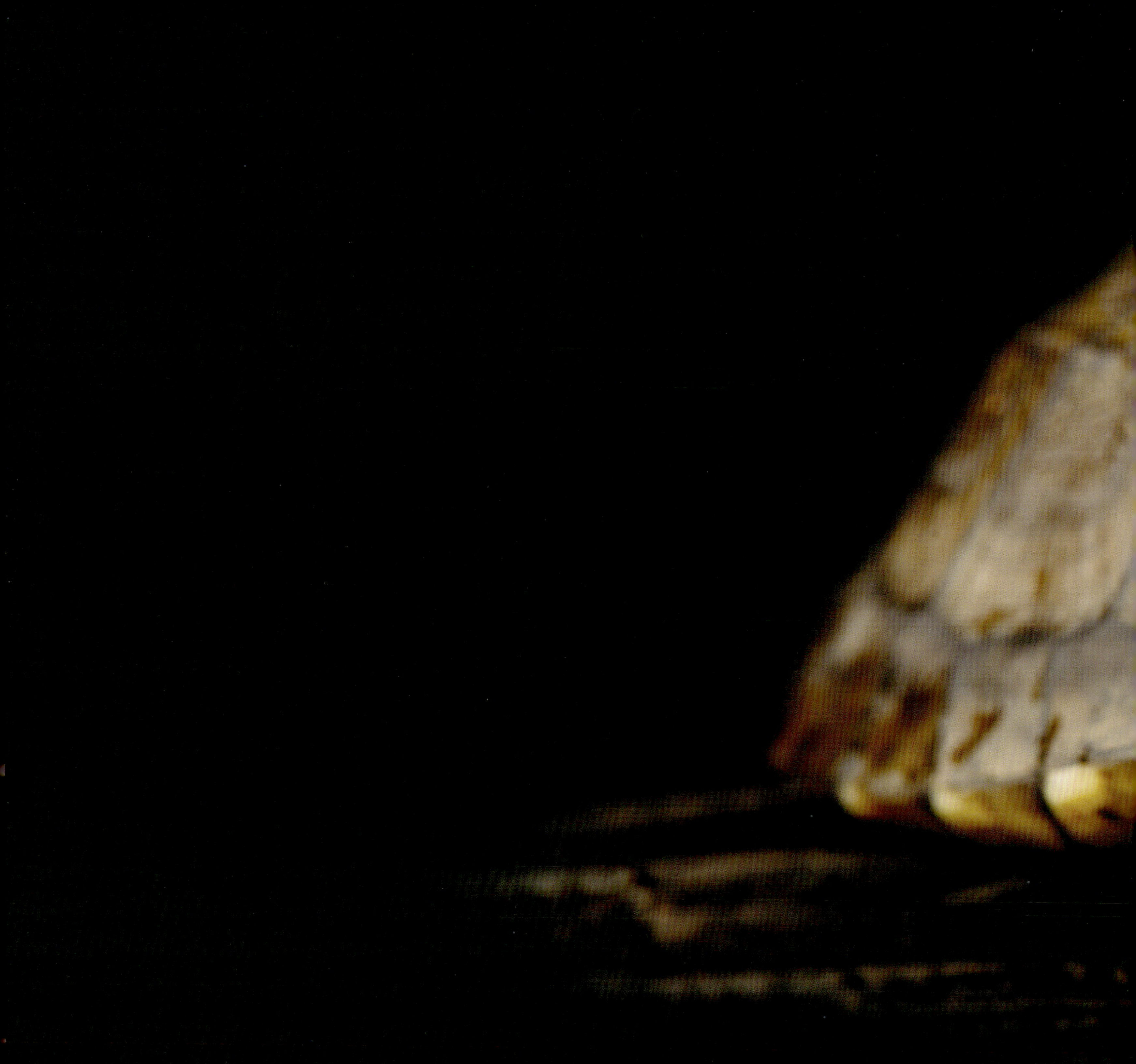

Scorpion Mud Turtle

Kinosternon scorpioides

CENTRAL AMERICA AND SOUTH AMERICA

Forest Crested Lizard

Calotes emma

ASIA

Baron's Green Racer

Philodryas baroni

SOUTH AMERICA

INDEX OF COMMON NAMES

Amazon Whipsnake 98
Argentinian Boa 46
Asian House Gecko 12
Asian Vine Snake 66
Banded Krait 150
Baron's Green Racer 204
Bent-toed gecko 90
Biak Tree Monitor 72
Black-and-white Tegu 152
Black Caiman 2
Black Mamba 26
Blue-legged Chameleon 68
Boomslang 62
Brahminy Blindsnake 142
Brown Anole 56
Cape Dwarf Chameleon 176
Carpet Python 168
Carrot-tail Viper Gecko 60
Chameleon Forest Dragon 38
Common Adder 88
Common Basilisk 182
Common Green Racer 164
Common Leopard Gecko 196
Cooper Creek Turtle 92
Cottonmouth 48
Crested Gecko 44
Day gecko 180
Dwarf Caiman 108
Eastern Bearded Dragon 64
Eastern Crevice-Skink 190
Eastern Spiny-tailed Gecko 118
European Glass Lizard 100
European Pond Turtle 170
Forest Crested Lizard 202
Freshwater Crocodile 52
Frilled Lizard 194
Frilly House Gecko 174
Gharial 140
Giant Horned Lizard 154
Green Anole 36
Green Iguana 80
Green Python 20
Green Rat Snake 158
Green Sea Turtle 30
Guyana Root Tegu 136
Halmahera Sailfin Dragon 162
Hermann's Tortoise 96
Indian Star Tortoise 84
Indochinese Spitting Cobra 104
Jackson's Chameleon 114
Komodo Dragon 18
Krefft's River Turtle 34
Kristin's Spiny-tailed Gecko 172
Lace Monitor 122
Madagascar Girdled Lizard 186
Malagasy Giant Hognose Snake 138
Mangrove Snake 74
Marine Iguana 22
Matamata Turtle 76
Mexican Horned Pit Viper 110
Muller's Skink 86
Namib Rock Agama 50
New Guinea Snake-Lizard 156
Nile Crocodile 10
Ornate Earless Agama 188
Painted Bronzeback 32
Panther Chameleon 40
Peringuey's Viper 128
Pig-nosed Turtle 178
Prickly Knob-tailed Gecko 134
Red-eared Slider 106
Red-eyed Crocodile Skink 130
Red-footed Tortoise 70
Red Worm Lizard 54
Rhinoceros Viper 116
Rough-scaled Brown Skink 199
Rough-scaled Python 102
Sand Boa 94
Santa Fe Iguana 112
Santa Fe Lava Lizard 14
Schmeltz's Rainbow Skink 148
Scorpion Mud Turtle 200
Shingleback 144
Southern African Python 132
Southern Leaf-tailed Gecko 8
Spear-point Leaf-tailed Gecko 28
Spectacled Caiman 16
Striped Kukri Snake 58
Sunda White-lipped Pit Viper 82
Thorn-tailed Gecko 184
Thorny Devil 166
Tokay Gecko 126
Tuatara 160
Veiled Chameleon 124
Wagler's Viper 6
Western Black Tree Snake 192
Western Diamondback Rattlesnake 24
White-lipped python 78
White-lipped Tree Viper 120
Yellow-lipped Sea Krait 42
Yellow Anaconda 146

INDEX OF SCIENTIFIC NAMES

Agama planiceps 50
Agkistrodon piscivorus 48
Ahaetulla prasina 66
Amblyrhynchus cristatus 22
Amphisbaena alba 54
Anolis carolinensis 36
Anolis sagrei 56
Aphaniotus ornata 188
Basiliscus basiliscus 182
Bitis nasicornis 116
Bitis peringueyi 128
Boiga dendrophila 74
Bradypodium pumilum 176
Bungarus fasciatus 150
Caiman crocodilus 16
Calotes emma 202
Calumma crypticum 68
Carettochelys insculpta 178
Carlia schmeltzii 148
Chamaeleo calyptratus 124
Chelonia mydas 30
Chelonoidis carbonaria 70
Chelus fimbriata 76
Chironius carinatus 98
Chlamydosaurus kingii 194
Conolophus pallidus 112
Correlophus ciliatus 44
Crocodylus johnstoni 52
Crocodylus niloticus 10
Crotalus atrox 24
Cyrtodactylus species 90
Dendrelaphis pictus 32
Dendroaspis polylepis 26
Dispholidus typus 62
Egernia mcpheei 190
Emydura kreffti 34
Emydura krefftii emmotti 92
Emys orbicularis 170
Epicrates alvarezi 46
Eryx colubrinus 94
Eublepharis macularius 196
Eunectes notaeus 146
Eutropis rudis 198
Furcifer pardalis 40
Gavialis gangeticus 140
Gekko gecko 126
Geochelone elegans 84
Gonocephalus chamaeleontinus 38
Gonysoma prasinum 158
Hemidactylus frenatus 12
Hemidactylus imbricatus 60
Hemidactylus platyurus 174
Hydrosaurus weberi 162
Iguana iguana 80
Indotyphlops braminus 142
Kinosternon scorpioides 200
Laticauda colubrina 42
Leioheterodon madagascariensis 138
Leiopython species 78
Lialis jicari 156
Loxopholis guianense 136
Melanosuchus niger 2
Microlophus barringtonensis 14
Moloch horridus 166
Morelia carinata 102
Morelia spilota mcdowelli 168
Morelia viridis 20
Naja siamensis 104
Nephrurus asper 134
Oligodon octolineatus 58
Ophryacus undulatus 110
Paleosuchus palpebrosus 108
Phelsuma sp. 180
Philodryas baroni 204
Philodryas viridissima 164
Phrynosoma asio 154
Pogona barbata 64
Pseudopus apodus 100
Python natalensis 132
Saltuarius swaini 8
Salvator merianae 152
Sphenodon punctatus 160
Sphenopmorphus muelleri 86
Strophurus assimilis 184
Strophurus krisalys 172
Strophurus williamsii 118
Testudo hermanni 96
Thrasops occidentalis 192
Tiliqua rugosa 144
Trachemys scripta elegans 106
Tribolonotus gracilis 130
Trimeresurus albolabris 120
Trimeresurus insularis 82
Trioceros jacksonii 114
Tropidolaemus wagleri 6
Uroplatus ebenaui 28
Varanus komodoensis 18
Varanus kordensis 72
Varanus varius 122
Vipera berus 88
Zonosaurus madagascariensis 186

First published in 2023 by Reed New Holland Publishers
Sydney

Level 1, 176 Fox Valley Road,
Wahroonga, NSW 2076, Australia

newhollandpublishers.com

A record of this book is held at the National Library of Australia.

ISBN 978 1 92554 667 5

Managing Director: Fiona Schultz
Publisher and Project Editor: Simon Papps
Designer: Andrew Davies
Production Director: Arlene Gippert

Printed in China

10 9 8 7 6 5 4 3 2 1

All images by Shutterstock.com, except for the photos on the following pages by Steve K. Wilson: pages 1, 6, 8, 12, 14, 32, 34, 52, 58, 64, 66, 82, 92, 102, 112, 118, 122, 128, 134, 144, 148, 168, 172, 174, 176, 184, 190, 198 and 202.